Prompted

1,600 Dystopian Writing Prompts

A Writer's Essential Resource

Prompted

1,600 Dystopian Writing Prompts

A Writer's Essential Resource

Iliana Barret

Prompted: 1,600 Dystopian Writing Prompts A Writer's Essential Resource© 2024 by Iliana Barret

ISBN: 9798327911895

Dedication:

For every writer feeling the block. You got this!

Introduction

Welcome to the realm of steampunk writing prompts—a portal to an alternate past, a stage for reimagining the Victorian era with a twist of futuristic technology, and a catalyst for weaving tales of steam-powered wonders and clockwork marvels. Within these pages, you'll traverse through a reimagined 19th century, breathing life into forgotten inventions, and resurrecting the spirits of intrepid inventors, daring adventurers, and mysterious automatons.

Unlocking Your Creativity In the vast tapestry of steampunk fiction, creativity knows no boundaries. It thrives in the gears and cogs of imagination, whispers in the hissing steam, and dances amidst the intricate machinery of innovation. Yet, even the most seasoned writers may find themselves ensnared in the clutches of writer's block, grappling with the challenge of bridging the chasm between past and fantastical present. Fear not, for within these prompts lie the seeds of inspiration, waiting to germinate in the fertile soil of your imagination. Whether you're crafting a saga of epic proportions or penning an intimate portrait of everyday life in a steampunk metropolis, these prompts are beacons of light, guiding you through the labyrinth of steampunk fiction and illuminating the path ahead.

Embracing the Steampunk Journey Writing steampunk fiction is a voyage—a pilgrimage to an alternate history, a quest to unearth the marvels of steam-powered technology, and a testament to the human spirit of innovation. With each stroke of the pen, we traverse through the corridors of this fantastical past, shedding light on forgotten inventions, and breathing life into characters long gone. Yet, like any journey, the path of steampunk fiction is fraught with challenges. There are days when inspiration flows like a mighty river, carrying us effortlessly through the gears of imagination. And then there are days when the well runs dry, when the clanks of machinery seem but a distant whisper, and the blank page taunts us with its silent reproach.

Finding Your Narrative Voice Amidst the trials and tribulations of steampunk fiction writing, lies a truth—a truth that transcends the boundaries of time and space. It is the truth of storytelling, of bearing witness to the human condition in a world powered by steam and innovation, and of finding your narrative voice amidst the cacophony of clanking gears and hissing steam. So let these prompts be your compass, your guiding star, and your faithful companion on the voyage of steampunk fiction writing. Let them inspire you to breathe life into forgotten inventions, to reimagine pivotal moments in this alternate history, and to give voice to the unsung inventors and adventurers of a steam-powered world. Before you embark on this odyssey through the annals of steampunk fiction, take a moment to consider how best to use this book. Approach each prompt with an open mind and a sense of curiosity. Experiment with different technological marvels, perspectives, and narrative styles, and let your imagination roam free across the vast expanse of this fantastical era. Above all, remember that writing steampunk fiction is a labor of love—a chance to commune with the spirits of innovation, and to leave your mark upon the annals of literary history. So embrace the journey, seize the reins of creativity, and let the writing begin.

100 Government and Authority Prompts

1. A totalitarian regime enforces absolute control over every aspect of life.
2. Citizens are monitored 24/7 by government-issued surveillance devices.
3. A society where dissent is punishable by exile to a desolate wasteland.
4. The government mandates daily public displays of loyalty and obedience.
5. A regime uses advanced technology to manipulate and control the population's thoughts.
6. A society where every citizen is assigned a role by the government at birth.
7. A dystopia where individual freedoms are sacrificed for the supposed greater good.
8. The government enforces a strict caste system, preventing social mobility.
9. A regime that uses fear and propaganda to maintain its grip on power.

10. Citizens are required to wear tracking devices that record their every move.
11. A society where the government controls the media and censors all dissent.
12. The government enforces a curfew, with severe penalties for violators.
13. A regime that uses mind control to maintain order and suppress rebellion.
14. Citizens are subjected to routine loyalty tests and interrogations.
15. The government enforces a policy of mandatory conscription for all young adults.
16. A society where the government controls reproduction and enforces population limits.
17. The regime uses genetic engineering to create a subservient class of citizens.
18. Citizens are required to report any suspicious behavior to the authorities.
19. A government that uses fear of external threats to justify its oppressive policies.
20. The regime uses advanced AI to predict and prevent potential rebellions.
21. Citizens are forced to undergo regular psychological evaluations to ensure loyalty.
22. A society where the government controls education and indoctrinates children.
23. The government enforces a policy of mandatory military service for all citizens.
24. A regime that uses brainwashing to ensure compliance and loyalty.

25. Citizens are required to participate in public displays of support for the regime.
26. The government enforces a policy of segregation based on social class.
27. A society where the government controls access to food and other essential resources.
28. The regime uses fear of disease to justify its oppressive policies.
29. Citizens are required to wear uniforms to promote conformity and obedience.
30. The government enforces a policy of mandatory surveillance for all citizens.
31. A regime that uses propaganda to manipulate public perception and control the narrative.
32. Citizens are subjected to routine searches and seizures by the authorities.
33. The government enforces a policy of strict censorship to suppress dissent.
34. A society where the government controls the economy and enforces strict regulations.
35. The regime uses fear of external enemies to justify its oppressive policies.
36. Citizens are required to pledge their loyalty to the regime on a daily basis.
37. The government enforces a policy of mandatory genetic testing for all citizens.
38. A regime that uses fear of rebellion to justify its oppressive policies.

39. Citizens are required to participate in government-mandated physical fitness programs.
40. The government enforces a policy of mandatory curfews and restrictions on movement.
41. A society where the government controls access to healthcare and other essential services.
42. The regime uses fear of internal threats to justify its oppressive policies.
43. Citizens are required to carry identification cards at all times.
44. The government enforces a policy of mandatory indoctrination for all citizens.
45. A regime that uses fear of disease to justify its oppressive policies.
46. Citizens are required to participate in government-mandated loyalty tests.
47. The government enforces a policy of mandatory surveillance for all citizens.
48. A society where the government controls the media and suppresses all dissent.
49. The regime uses fear of rebellion to justify its oppressive policies.
50. Citizens are required to wear tracking devices that record their every move.
51. The government enforces a policy of mandatory conscription for all young adults.
52. A regime that uses brainwashing to ensure compliance and loyalty.

53. Citizens are required to participate in public displays of support for the regime.
54. The government enforces a policy of segregation based on social class.
55. A society where the government controls access to food and other essential resources.
56. The regime uses fear of disease to justify its oppressive policies.
57. Citizens are required to wear uniforms to promote conformity and obedience.
58. The government enforces a policy of mandatory surveillance for all citizens.
59. A regime that uses propaganda to manipulate public perception and control the narrative.
60. Citizens are subjected to routine searches and seizures by the authorities.
61. The government enforces a policy of strict censorship to suppress dissent.
62. A society where the government controls the economy and enforces strict regulations.
63. The regime uses fear of external enemies to justify its oppressive policies.
64. Citizens are required to pledge their loyalty to the regime on a daily basis.
65. The government enforces a policy of mandatory genetic testing for all citizens.
66. A regime that uses fear of rebellion to justify its oppressive policies.

67. Citizens are required to participate in government-mandated physical fitness programs.
68. The government enforces a policy of mandatory curfews and restrictions on movement.
69. A society where the government controls access to healthcare and other essential services.
70. The regime uses fear of internal threats to justify its oppressive policies.
71. Citizens are required to carry identification cards at all times.
72. The government enforces a policy of mandatory indoctrination for all citizens.
73. A regime that uses fear of disease to justify its oppressive policies.
74. Citizens are required to participate in government-mandated loyalty tests.
75. The government enforces a policy of mandatory surveillance for all citizens.
76. A society where the government controls the media and suppresses all dissent.
77. The regime uses fear of rebellion to justify its oppressive policies.
78. Citizens are required to wear tracking devices that record their every move.
79. The government enforces a policy of mandatory conscription for all young adults.
80. A regime that uses brainwashing to ensure compliance and loyalty.

81. Citizens are required to participate in public displays of support for the regime.
82. The government enforces a policy of segregation based on social class.
83. A society where the government controls access to food and other essential resources.
84. The regime uses fear of disease to justify its oppressive policies.
85. Citizens are required to wear uniforms to promote conformity and obedience.
86. The government enforces a policy of mandatory surveillance for all citizens.
87. A regime that uses propaganda to manipulate public perception and control the narrative.
88. Citizens are subjected to routine searches and seizures by the authorities.
89. The government enforces a policy of strict censorship to suppress dissent.
90. A society where the government controls the economy and enforces strict regulations.
91. The regime uses fear of external enemies to justify its oppressive policies.
92. Citizens are required to pledge their loyalty to the regime on a daily basis.
93. The government enforces a policy of mandatory genetic testing for all citizens.
94. A regime that uses fear of rebellion to justify its oppressive policies.

95. Citizens are required to participate in government-mandated physical fitness programs.
96. The government enforces a policy of mandatory curfews and restrictions on movement.
97. A society where the government controls access to healthcare and other essential services.
98. The regime uses fear of internal threats to justify its oppressive policies.
99. Citizens are required to carry identification cards at all times.
100. The government enforces a policy of mandatory indoctrination for all citizens.

100 Environmental Collapse Prompts

1. The world is ravaged by climate change, leading to extreme weather events and food shortages.
2. A society where clean water is a luxury only the wealthy can afford.
3. The environment is so toxic that people must wear protective gear at all times.
4. A dystopia where natural disasters have become a daily occurrence.
5. The government enforces strict regulations on resource consumption due to scarcity.
6. A society where the oceans have risen, submerging coastal cities.
7. The air is so polluted that breathing without a mask is fatal.
8. A dystopia where deforestation has led to a lack of oxygen and severe climate changes.
9. The world is plagued by drought, making water the most valuable commodity.

10. A society where animals have become extinct due to environmental degradation.
11. The government enforces population control to manage scarce resources.
12. A dystopia where the soil is too contaminated to grow crops.
13. The environment is so unstable that earthquakes and volcanic eruptions are common.
14. A society where people live in domed cities to escape the harsh environment.
15. The government enforces a ban on all fossil fuels to combat environmental collapse.
16. A dystopia where the sun is permanently obscured by pollution.
17. The world is plagued by toxic waste, making large areas uninhabitable.
18. A society where people must grow their own food due to supply chain collapse.
19. The government enforces strict recycling laws to combat waste.
20. A dystopia where the climate is so unpredictable that seasons no longer exist.
21. The world is ravaged by wildfires, destroying homes and forests.
22. A society where air quality is so poor that respiratory diseases are rampant.
23. The government enforces rationing of essential resources like water and food.
24. A dystopia where acid rain destroys crops and buildings.

25. The environment is so degraded that natural beauty is a distant memory.
26. A society where people must migrate constantly to find livable conditions.
27. The government enforces a ban on all single-use plastics.
28. A dystopia where the oceans are so polluted that marine life is extinct.
29. The world is plagued by superstorms that devastate entire regions.
30. A society where people live underground to escape the harsh surface conditions.
31. The government enforces a policy of reforestation to combat environmental collapse.
32. A dystopia where the land is so barren that desertification is widespread.
33. The environment is so unstable that natural disasters are common.
34. A society where the rich live in climate-controlled enclaves while the poor suffer.
35. The government enforces strict emissions regulations to combat air pollution.
36. A dystopia where the ice caps have melted, leading to catastrophic sea-level rise.
37. The world is plagued by toxic smog that makes visibility near zero.
38. A society where people must purify their own water due to contamination.
39. The government enforces a policy of zero waste to combat environmental collapse.

40. A dystopia where the forests are gone, leading to severe climate changes.
41. The environment is so toxic that people cannot go outside without protection.
42. A society where people must ration their own food due to shortages.
43. The government enforces a ban on all non-renewable energy sources.
44. A dystopia where the climate is so harsh that survival is a daily struggle.
45. The world is plagued by environmental refugees fleeing uninhabitable regions.
46. A society where people must live in eco-friendly homes to reduce their impact.
47. The government enforces a policy of renewable energy to combat environmental collapse.
48. A dystopia where the air is so polluted that blue skies are a distant memory.
49. The environment is so unstable that natural disasters are common.
50. A society where the government controls access to clean water.
51. The government enforces a policy of conservation to combat resource scarcity.
52. A dystopia where the land is so contaminated that farming is impossible.
53. The world is plagued by environmental toxins that cause widespread disease.
54. A society where people must wear protective gear to go outside.

55. The government enforces strict laws on resource consumption.
56. A dystopia where the environment is so harsh that survival is a daily struggle.
57. The world is ravaged by climate change, leading to extreme weather events.
58. A society where clean water is a luxury only the wealthy can afford.
59. The environment is so toxic that people must wear protective gear at all times.
60. A dystopia where natural disasters have become a daily occurrence.
61. The government enforces strict regulations on resource consumption due to scarcity.
62. A society where the oceans have risen, submerging coastal cities.
63. The air is so polluted that breathing without a mask is fatal.
64. A dystopia where deforestation has led to a lack of oxygen and severe climate changes.
65. The world is plagued by drought, making water the most valuable commodity.
66. A society where animals have become extinct due to environmental degradation.
67. The government enforces population control to manage scarce resources.
68. A dystopia where the soil is too contaminated to grow crops.
69. The environment is so unstable that earthquakes and volcanic eruptions are common.

70. A society where people live in domed cities to escape the harsh environment.
71. The government enforces a ban on all fossil fuels to combat environmental collapse.
72. A dystopia where the sun is permanently obscured by pollution.
73. The world is plagued by toxic waste, making large areas uninhabitable.
74. A society where people must grow their own food due to supply chain collapse.
75. The government enforces strict recycling laws to combat waste.
76. A dystopia where the climate is so unpredictable that seasons no longer exist.
77. The world is ravaged by wildfires, destroying homes and forests.
78. A society where air quality is so poor that respiratory diseases are rampant.
79. The government enforces rationing of essential resources like water and food.
80. A dystopia where acid rain destroys crops and buildings.
81. The environment is so degraded that natural beauty is a distant memory.
82. A society where people must migrate constantly to find livable conditions.
83. The government enforces a ban on all single-use plastics.
84. A dystopia where the oceans are so polluted that marine life is extinct.

85. The world is plagued by superstorms that devastate entire regions.
86. A society where people live underground to escape the harsh surface conditions.
87. The government enforces a policy of reforestation to combat environmental collapse.
88. A dystopia where the land is so barren that desertification is widespread.
89. The environment is so unstable that natural disasters are common.
90. A society where the rich live in climate-controlled enclaves while the poor suffer.
91. The government enforces strict emissions regulations to combat air pollution.
92. A dystopia where the ice caps have melted, leading to catastrophic sea-level rise.
93. The world is plagued by toxic smog that makes visibility near zero.
94. A society where people must purify their own water due to contamination.
95. The government enforces a policy of zero waste to combat environmental collapse.
96. A dystopia where the forests are gone, leading to severe climate changes.
97. The environment is so toxic that people cannot go outside without protection.
98. A society where people must ration their own food due to shortages.
99. The government enforces a ban on all non-renewable energy sources.

100.   A dystopia where the climate is so harsh that survival is a daily struggle.

100 Government and Authority Prompts

1. A dystopia where AI governs every aspect of human life.
2. The government uses advanced technology to control and manipulate the population.
3. A society where people are implanted with chips that monitor their thoughts and actions.
4. A dystopia where virtual reality is used to pacify and distract the population.
5. The government enforces a ban on all technology not approved by the state.
6. A society where humans are replaced by robots in most jobs.
7. The government uses drones to monitor and control the population.
8. A dystopia where people are required to undergo regular mind scans to ensure loyalty.
9. The government enforces strict regulations on the use of technology.

10. A society where technology is used to create a surveillance state.
11. The government uses biometric data to control access to resources and services.
12. A dystopia where people are forced to live in smart cities controlled by AI.
13. The government enforces a policy of mandatory technology use.
14. A society where technology is used to manipulate and control emotions.
15. The government uses facial recognition to monitor and control the population.
16. A dystopia where people are required to wear devices that track their every move.
17. The government enforces a ban on all forms of digital communication.
18. A society where technology is used to enforce strict social hierarchies.
19. The government uses AI to predict and prevent crime.
20. A dystopia where people are controlled by implants that regulate their behavior.
21. The government enforces a policy of mandatory biometric identification.
22. A society where technology is used to enforce conformity and obedience.
23. The government uses AI to monitor and control the media.
24. A dystopia where people are required to undergo regular brainwashing sessions.

25. The government enforces strict regulations on the use of AI.
26. A society where technology is used to control and manipulate memories.
27. The government uses drones to enforce curfews and restrictions on movement.
28. A dystopia where people are implanted with devices that control their actions.
29. The government enforces a policy of mandatory digital surveillance.
30. A society where technology is used to suppress dissent and rebellion.
31. The government uses AI to control access to food and other essential resources.
32. A dystopia where people are required to undergo regular loyalty tests.
33. The government enforces strict regulations on the use of digital currency.
34. A society where technology is used to enforce strict population control.
35. The government uses biometric data to track and control the population.
36. A dystopia where people are forced to live in controlled environments.
37. The government enforces a policy of mandatory mind control technology.
38. A society where technology is used to manipulate and control thoughts.
39. The government uses AI to monitor and control all forms of communication.

40. A dystopia where people are required to wear devices that control their emotions.
41. The government enforces a ban on all forms of independent technology development.
42. A society where technology is used to enforce strict social order.
43. The government uses drones to monitor and control all public spaces.
44. A dystopia where people are implanted with devices that track their every thought.
45. The government enforces a policy of mandatory digital identification.
46. A society where technology is used to control and manipulate behavior.
47. The government uses AI to predict and prevent potential threats.
48. A dystopia where people are required to undergo regular brain scans.
49. The government enforces strict regulations on the use of digital technology.
50. A society where technology is used to enforce strict conformity.
51. The government uses biometric data to control access to all services.
52. A dystopia where people are implanted with devices that control their behavior.
53. The government enforces a policy of mandatory technology use.
54. A society where technology is used to manipulate and control memories.

55. The government uses AI to monitor and control all forms of communication.
56. A dystopia where people are required to wear devices that track their every move.
57. The government enforces a ban on all forms of digital communication.
58. A society where technology is used to enforce strict social hierarchies.
59. The government uses AI to predict and prevent crime.
60. A dystopia where people are controlled by implants that regulate their behavior.
61. The government enforces a policy of mandatory biometric identification.
62. A society where technology is used to enforce conformity and obedience.
63. The government uses AI to monitor and control the media.
64. A dystopia where people are required to undergo regular brainwashing sessions.
65. The government enforces strict regulations on the use of AI.
66. A society where technology is used to control and manipulate memories.
67. The government uses drones to enforce curfews and restrictions on movement.
68. A dystopia where people are implanted with devices that control their actions.
69. The government enforces a policy of mandatory digital surveillance.

70. A society where technology is used to suppress dissent and rebellion.
71. The government uses AI to control access to food and other essential resources.
72. A dystopia where people are required to undergo regular loyalty tests.
73. The government enforces strict regulations on the use of digital currency.
74. A society where technology is used to enforce strict population control.
75. The government uses biometric data to track and control the population.
76. A dystopia where people are forced to live in controlled environments.
77. The government enforces a policy of mandatory mind control technology.
78. A society where technology is used to manipulate and control thoughts.
79. The government uses AI to monitor and control all forms of communication.
80. A dystopia where people are required to wear devices that control their emotions.
81. The government enforces a ban on all forms of independent technology development.
82. A society where technology is used to enforce strict social order.
83. The government uses drones to monitor and control all public spaces.
84. A dystopia where people are implanted with devices that track their every thought.

85. The government enforces a policy of mandatory digital identification.
86. A society where technology is used to control and manipulate behavior.
87. The government uses AI to predict and prevent potential threats.
88. A dystopia where people are required to undergo regular brain scans.
89. The government enforces strict regulations on the use of digital technology.
90. A society where technology is used to enforce strict conformity.
91. The government uses biometric data to control access to all services.
92. A dystopia where people are implanted with devices that control their behavior.
93. The government enforces a policy of mandatory technology use.
94. A society where technology is used to manipulate and control memories.
95. The government uses AI to monitor and control all forms of communication.
96. A dystopia where people are required to wear devices that track their every move.
97. The government enforces a ban on all forms of digital communication.
98. A society where technology is used to enforce strict social hierarchies.
99. The government uses AI to predict and prevent crime.

100.   A dystopia where people are controlled by implants that regulate their behavior.

100 Societal Collapse Prompts

1. A society where the economy has collapsed, leading to widespread poverty and unrest.
2. A dystopia where the government has fallen, and lawlessness reigns.
3. A society where basic services like healthcare and education no longer exist.
4. A dystopia where food shortages have led to widespread famine.
5. A society where the infrastructure has crumbled, making travel and communication difficult.
6. A dystopia where the collapse of the power grid has left the world in darkness.
7. A society where disease and illness are rampant due to lack of healthcare.
8. A dystopia where the collapse of the government has led to civil war.
9. A society where the rich have retreated to fortified enclaves, leaving the poor to fend for themselves.
10. A dystopia where the collapse of the economy has led to widespread crime and violence.

11. A society where the collapse of the education system has left a generation uneducated.
12. A dystopia where the collapse of the healthcare system has led to widespread death and suffering.
13. A society where the collapse of the transportation system has made travel impossible.
14. A dystopia where the collapse of the government has led to the rise of warlords.
15. A society where the collapse of the economy has led to a barter system.
16. A dystopia where the collapse of the power grid has led to widespread chaos.
17. A society where disease and illness are rampant due to lack of clean water.
18. A dystopia where the collapse of the government has led to widespread anarchy.
19. A society where the rich live in luxury while the poor live in squalor.
20. A dystopia where the collapse of the economy has led to widespread homelessness.
21. A society where the collapse of the education system has led to widespread ignorance.
22. A dystopia where the collapse of the healthcare system has led to widespread despair.
23. A society where the collapse of the transportation system has led to isolation.
24. A dystopia where the collapse of the government has led to the rise of militias.
25. A society where the collapse of the economy has led to widespread hunger.

26. A dystopia where the collapse of the power grid has led to widespread fear.
27. A society where disease and illness are rampant due to lack of sanitation.
28. A dystopia where the collapse of the government has led to the rise of gangs.
29. A society where the rich exploit the poor for their own gain.
30. A dystopia where the collapse of the economy has led to widespread despair.
31. A society where the collapse of the education system has led to widespread illiteracy.
32. A dystopia where the collapse of the healthcare system has led to widespread suffering.
33. A society where the collapse of the transportation system has led to isolation and despair.
34. A dystopia where the collapse of the government has led to the rise of criminal organizations.
35. A society where the collapse of the economy has led to widespread desperation.
36. A dystopia where the collapse of the power grid has led to widespread lawlessness.
37. A society where disease and illness are rampant due to lack of resources.
38. A dystopia where the collapse of the government has led to widespread chaos and violence.
39. A society where the rich live in fortified enclaves while the poor live in fear.
40. A dystopia where the collapse of the economy has led to widespread poverty.

41. A society where the collapse of the education system has led to widespread ignorance and fear.
42. A dystopia where the collapse of the healthcare system has led to widespread death and disease.
43. A society where the collapse of the transportation system has led to isolation and despair.
44. A dystopia where the collapse of the government has led to the rise of ruthless leaders.
45. A society where the collapse of the economy has led to widespread hunger and suffering.
46. A dystopia where the collapse of the power grid has led to widespread panic.
47. A society where disease and illness are rampant due to lack of clean water and sanitation.
48. A dystopia where the collapse of the government has led to widespread anarchy and violence.
49. A society where the rich exploit the poor for their own gain and live in luxury.
50. A dystopia where the collapse of the economy has led to widespread despair and hopelessness.
51. A society where the collapse of the education system has led to widespread ignorance and fear.
52. A dystopia where the collapse of the healthcare system has led to widespread suffering and death.
53. A society where the collapse of the transportation system has led to isolation and despair.
54. A dystopia where the collapse of the government has led to the rise of criminal organizations.
55. A society where the collapse of the economy has led to widespread desperation and crime.

56. A dystopia where the collapse of the power grid has led to widespread lawlessness and fear.
57. A society where disease and illness are rampant due to lack of resources and healthcare.
58. A dystopia where the collapse of the government has led to widespread chaos and violence.
59. A society where the rich live in fortified enclaves while the poor live in fear and suffering.
60. A dystopia where the collapse of the economy has led to widespread poverty and hunger.
61. A society where the collapse of the education system has led to widespread ignorance and despair.
62. A dystopia where the collapse of the healthcare system has led to widespread death and disease.
63. A society where the collapse of the transportation system has led to isolation and despair.
64. A dystopia where the collapse of the government has led to the rise of ruthless leaders and warlords.
65. A society where the collapse of the economy has led to widespread hunger and suffering.
66. A dystopia where the collapse of the power grid has led to widespread panic and fear.
67. A society where disease and illness are rampant due to lack of clean water and sanitation.
68. A dystopia where the collapse of the government has led to widespread anarchy and violence.
69. A society where the rich exploit the poor for their own gain and live in luxury.
70. A dystopia where the collapse of the economy has led to widespread despair and hopelessness.

71. A society where the collapse of the education system has led to widespread ignorance and fear.
72. A dystopia where the collapse of the healthcare system has led to widespread suffering and death.
73. A society where the collapse of the transportation system has led to isolation and despair.
74. A dystopia where the collapse of the government has led to the rise of criminal organizations.
75. A society where the collapse of the economy has led to widespread desperation and crime.
76. A dystopia where the collapse of the power grid has led to widespread lawlessness and fear.
77. A society where disease and illness are rampant due to lack of resources and healthcare.
78. A dystopia where the collapse of the government has led to widespread chaos and violence.
79. A society where the rich live in fortified enclaves while the poor live in fear and suffering.
80. A dystopia where the collapse of the economy has led to widespread poverty and hunger.
81. A society where the collapse of the education system has led to widespread ignorance and despair.
82. A dystopia where the collapse of the healthcare system has led to widespread death and disease.
83. A society where the collapse of the transportation system has led to isolation and despair.
84. A dystopia where the collapse of the government has led to the rise of ruthless leaders and warlords.
85. A society where the collapse of the economy has led to widespread hunger and suffering.

86. A dystopia where the collapse of the power grid has led to widespread panic and fear.
87. A society where disease and illness are rampant due to lack of clean water and sanitation.
88. A dystopia where the collapse of the government has led to widespread anarchy and violence.
89. A society where the rich exploit the poor for their own gain and live in luxury.
90. A dystopia where the collapse of the economy has led to widespread despair and hopelessness.
91. A society where the collapse of the education system has led to widespread ignorance and fear.
92. A dystopia where the collapse of the healthcare system has led to widespread suffering and death.
93. A society where the collapse of the transportation system has led to isolation and despair.
94. A dystopia where the collapse of the government has led to the rise of criminal organizations.
95. A society where the collapse of the economy has led to widespread desperation and crime.
96. A dystopia where the collapse of the power grid has led to widespread lawlessness and fear.
97. A society where disease and illness are rampant due to lack of resources and healthcare.
98. A dystopia where the collapse of the government has led to widespread chaos and violence.
99. A society where the rich live in fortified enclaves while the poor live in fear and suffering.
100. A dystopia where the collapse of the economy has led to widespread poverty and hunger.

100 Post-Apocalyptic Prompts

1. The world is devastated by a nuclear apocalypse, leaving few survivors.
2. A society where people must scavenge for resources in a wasteland.
3. A dystopia where the world is overrun by mutated creatures.
4. The government collapses, and survivors form tribes to protect themselves.
5. A society where people must defend themselves against raiders and bandits.
6. A dystopia where the world is covered in toxic waste, making survival difficult.
7. The environment is so harsh that only the strongest can survive.
8. A society where people must find a way to rebuild after a global catastrophe.
9. A dystopia where survivors live in underground bunkers to escape the surface.
10. The world is plagued by radiation, making large areas uninhabitable.

11. A society where people must rely on ancient technology to survive.
12. A dystopia where the world is covered in ash and smoke from volcanic eruptions.
13. The government collapses, and survivors form alliances to protect themselves.
14. A society where people must find a way to purify water to survive.
15. A dystopia where the world is frozen, and survival depends on finding warmth.
16. The world is devastated by a massive asteroid impact, leaving few survivors.
17. A society where people must hunt for food in a barren wasteland.
18. A dystopia where the world is overrun by deadly viruses.
19. The government collapses, and survivors form communities to protect themselves.
20. A society where people must find a way to generate power to survive.
21. A dystopia where the world is covered in darkness, and survival depends on finding light.
22. The world is devastated by a supervolcano eruption, leaving few survivors.
23. A society where people must find a way to grow food in a barren wasteland.
24. A dystopia where the world is overrun by hostile alien species.
25. The government collapses, and survivors form militias to protect themselves.

26. A society where people must find a way to purify air to survive.
27. A dystopia where the world is flooded, and survival depends on finding dry land.
28. The world is devastated by a global pandemic, leaving few survivors.
29. A society where people must find a way to communicate in a disconnected world.
30. A dystopia where the world is overrun by rogue AI.
31. The government collapses, and survivors form coalitions to protect themselves.
32. A society where people must find a way to rebuild infrastructure to survive.
33. A dystopia where the world is covered in sand, and survival depends on finding water.
34. The world is devastated by a massive solar flare, leaving few survivors.
35. A society where people must find a way to repair technology to survive.
36. A dystopia where the world is overrun by zombie-like creatures.
37. The government collapses, and survivors form factions to protect themselves.
38. A society where people must find a way to create shelter to survive.
39. A dystopia where the world is covered in toxic fog, making survival difficult.
40. The world is devastated by a global war, leaving few survivors.

41. A society where people must find a way to navigate a desolate landscape.
42. A dystopia where the world is overrun by superhuman beings.
43. The government collapses, and survivors form clans to protect themselves.
44. A society where people must find a way to repair damaged ecosystems to survive.
45. A dystopia where the world is covered in radiation, making survival difficult.
46. The world is devastated by a massive earthquake, leaving few survivors.
47. A society where people must find a way to communicate in a disconnected world.
48. A dystopia where the world is overrun by deadly fungi.
49. The government collapses, and survivors form alliances to protect themselves.
50. A society where people must find a way to generate power to survive.
51. A dystopia where the world is covered in darkness, and survival depends on finding light.
52. The world is devastated by a supervolcano eruption, leaving few survivors.
53. A society where people must find a way to grow food in a barren wasteland.
54. A dystopia where the world is overrun by hostile alien species.
55. The government collapses, and survivors form militias to protect themselves.

56. A society where people must find a way to purify air to survive.
57. A dystopia where the world is flooded, and survival depends on finding dry land.
58. The world is devastated by a global pandemic, leaving few survivors.
59. A society where people must find a way to communicate in a disconnected world.
60. A dystopia where the world is overrun by rogue AI.
61. The government collapses, and survivors form coalitions to protect themselves.
62. A society where people must find a way to rebuild infrastructure to survive.
63. A dystopia where the world is covered in sand, and survival depends on finding water.
64. The world is devastated by a massive solar flare, leaving few survivors.
65. A society where people must find a way to repair technology to survive.
66. A dystopia where the world is overrun by zombie-like creatures.
67. The government collapses, and survivors form factions to protect themselves.
68. A society where people must find a way to create shelter to survive.
69. A dystopia where the world is covered in toxic fog, making survival difficult.
70. The world is devastated by a global war, leaving few survivors.

71. A society where people must find a way to navigate a desolate landscape.
72. A dystopia where the world is overrun by superhuman beings.
73. The government collapses, and survivors form clans to protect themselves.
74. A society where people must find a way to repair damaged ecosystems to survive.
75. A dystopia where the world is covered in radiation, making survival difficult.
76. The world is devastated by a massive earthquake, leaving few survivors.
77. A society where people must find a way to communicate in a disconnected world.
78. A dystopia where the world is overrun by deadly fungi.
79. The government collapses, and survivors form alliances to protect themselves.
80. A society where people must find a way to generate power to survive.
81. A dystopia where the world is covered in darkness, and survival depends on finding light.
82. The world is devastated by a supervolcano eruption, leaving few survivors.
83. A society where people must find a way to grow food in a barren wasteland.
84. A dystopia where the world is overrun by hostile alien species.
85. The government collapses, and survivors form militias to protect themselves.

86. A society where people must find a way to purify air to survive.
87. A dystopia where the world is flooded, and survival depends on finding dry land.
88. The world is devastated by a global pandemic, leaving few survivors.
89. A society where people must find a way to communicate in a disconnected world.
90. A dystopia where the world is overrun by rogue AI.
91. The government collapses, and survivors form coalitions to protect themselves.
92. A society where people must find a way to rebuild infrastructure to survive.
93. A dystopia where the world is covered in sand, and survival depends on finding water.
94. The world is devastated by a massive solar flare, leaving few survivors.
95. A society where people must find a way to repair technology to survive.
96. A dystopia where the world is overrun by zombie-like creatures.
97. The government collapses, and survivors form factions to protect themselves.
98. A society where people must find a way to create shelter to survive.
99. A dystopia where the world is covered in toxic fog, making survival difficult.
100. The world is devastated by a global war, leaving few survivors.

100 Medical and Genetic Manipulation Prompts

1. A society where genetic engineering is used to create a perfect race.
2. A dystopia where only the genetically modified are allowed to have children.
3. The government enforces a policy of mandatory genetic testing.
4. A society where people are divided based on their genetic purity.
5. A dystopia where the government controls all genetic research.
6. A society where genetic enhancements are a requirement for certain jobs.
7. The government enforces a ban on all natural reproduction.
8. A dystopia where people are genetically engineered for specific tasks.
9. A society where genetic manipulation is used to create super soldiers.

10. The government enforces a policy of mandatory genetic modifications.
11. A dystopia where genetic defects are punishable by exile.
12. A society where the government controls access to genetic enhancements.
13. A dystopia where people are required to undergo regular genetic testing.
14. The government enforces a ban on all non-approved genetic modifications.
15. A society where genetic manipulation is used to control behavior.
16. A dystopia where the government uses genetic engineering to create a subservient class.
17. A society where people are genetically modified to be more productive.
18. The government enforces a policy of mandatory genetic enhancements.
19. A dystopia where genetic manipulation is used to suppress dissent.
20. A society where people are genetically engineered to be more obedient.
21. The government enforces a ban on all non-approved genetic research.
22. A dystopia where genetic defects are punishable by imprisonment.
23. A society where the government controls access to genetic technology.
24. A dystopia where people are required to undergo regular genetic modifications.

25. The government enforces a policy of mandatory genetic testing.
26. A society where genetic manipulation is used to control reproduction.
27. A dystopia where the government uses genetic engineering to create a docile population.
28. A society where people are genetically modified to be more intelligent.
29. The government enforces a policy of mandatory genetic enhancements.
30. A dystopia where genetic manipulation is used to enforce conformity.
31. A society where people are genetically engineered to be more compliant.
32. The government enforces a ban on all non-approved genetic modifications.
33. A dystopia where genetic defects are punishable by exile or death.
34. A society where the government controls access to genetic technology.
35. A dystopia where people are required to undergo regular genetic testing.
36. The government enforces a policy of mandatory genetic modifications.
37. A society where genetic manipulation is used to control behavior and thoughts.
38. A dystopia where the government uses genetic engineering to create a subservient class.
39. A society where people are genetically modified to be more productive and efficient.

40. The government enforces a policy of mandatory genetic enhancements.
41. A dystopia where genetic manipulation is used to suppress dissent and rebellion.
42. A society where people are genetically engineered to be more obedient and compliant.
43. The government enforces a ban on all non-approved genetic research and modifications.
44. A dystopia where genetic defects are punishable by imprisonment or death.
45. A society where the government controls access to genetic technology and enhancements.
46. A dystopia where people are required to undergo regular genetic modifications and testing.
47. The government enforces a policy of mandatory genetic enhancements for all citizens.
48. A society where genetic manipulation is used to control reproduction and population growth.
49. A dystopia where the government uses genetic engineering to create a docile and compliant population.
50. A society where people are genetically modified to be more intelligent and efficient.
51. The government enforces a policy of mandatory genetic testing and enhancements.
52. A dystopia where genetic manipulation is used to enforce conformity and obedience.
53. A society where people are genetically engineered to be more compliant and obedient.
54. The government enforces a ban on all non-approved genetic research and modifications.

55. A dystopia where genetic defects are punishable by exile or death.
56. A society where the government controls access to genetic technology and enhancements.
57. A dystopia where people are required to undergo regular genetic modifications and testing.
58. The government enforces a policy of mandatory genetic enhancements for all citizens.
59. A society where genetic manipulation is used to control behavior and thoughts.
60. A dystopia where the government uses genetic engineering to create a subservient class.
61. A society where people are genetically modified to be more productive and efficient.
62. The government enforces a policy of mandatory genetic enhancements.
63. A dystopia where genetic manipulation is used to suppress dissent and rebellion.
64. A society where people are genetically engineered to be more obedient and compliant.
65. The government enforces a ban on all non-approved genetic research and modifications.
66. A dystopia where genetic defects are punishable by imprisonment or death.
67. A society where the government controls access to genetic technology and enhancements.
68. A dystopia where people are required to undergo regular genetic modifications and testing.
69. The government enforces a policy of mandatory genetic enhancements for all citizens.

70. A society where genetic manipulation is used to control reproduction and population growth.
71. A dystopia where the government uses genetic engineering to create a docile and compliant population.
72. A society where people are genetically modified to be more intelligent and efficient.
73. The government enforces a policy of mandatory genetic testing and enhancements.
74. A dystopia where genetic manipulation is used to enforce conformity and obedience.
75. A society where people are genetically engineered to be more compliant and obedient.
76. The government enforces a ban on all non-approved genetic research and modifications.
77. A dystopia where genetic defects are punishable by exile or death.
78. A society where the government controls access to genetic technology and enhancements.
79. A dystopia where people are required to undergo regular genetic modifications and testing.
80. The government enforces a policy of mandatory genetic enhancements for all citizens.
81. A society where genetic manipulation is used to control behavior and thoughts.
82. A dystopia where the government uses genetic engineering to create a subservient class.
83. A society where people are genetically modified to be more productive and efficient.
84. The government enforces a policy of mandatory genetic enhancements.

85. A dystopia where genetic manipulation is used to suppress dissent and rebellion.
86. A society where people are genetically engineered to be more obedient and compliant.
87. The government enforces a ban on all non-approved genetic research and modifications.
88. A dystopia where genetic defects are punishable by imprisonment or death.
89. A society where the government controls access to genetic technology and enhancements.
90. A dystopia where people are required to undergo regular genetic modifications and testing.
91. The government enforces a policy of mandatory genetic enhancements for all citizens.
92. A society where genetic manipulation is used to control reproduction and population growth.
93. A dystopia where the government uses genetic engineering to create a docile and compliant population.
94. A society where people are genetically modified to be more intelligent and efficient.
95. The government enforces a policy of mandatory genetic testing and enhancements.
96. A dystopia where genetic manipulation is used to enforce conformity and obedience.
97. A society where people are genetically engineered to be more compliant and obedient.
98. The government enforces a ban on all non-approved genetic research and modifications.
99. A dystopia where genetic defects are punishable by exile or death.

100. A society where the government controls access to genetic technology and enhancements.

100 Social Hierarchies and Inequality Prompts

1. A society where the rich live in luxury while the poor live in squalor.
2. A dystopia where the government enforces strict social hierarchies.
3. A society where people are divided based on their social class.
4. A dystopia where the rich have all the power and control.
5. A society where the poor are forced to work in dangerous conditions.
6. A dystopia where social mobility is impossible.
7. A society where the rich live in fortified enclaves.
8. A dystopia where the poor are denied basic rights.
9. A society where the rich exploit the poor for their own gain.
10. A dystopia where the government enforces strict caste systems.
11. A society where the poor are forced to serve the rich.

12. A dystopia where social class determines access to resources.
13. A society where the rich live in luxury while the poor struggle to survive.
14. A dystopia where the government enforces strict social order.
15. A society where the poor are denied access to education and healthcare.
16. A dystopia where the rich control all aspects of society.
17. A society where the poor are forced to work in labor camps.
18. A dystopia where social class determines your fate.
19. A society where the rich live in opulence while the poor live in poverty.
20. A dystopia where the government enforces strict social segregation.
21. A society where the poor are denied access to clean water and food.
22. A dystopia where the rich have all the privileges and rights.
23. A society where the poor are forced to live in slums.
24. A dystopia where social class determines access to opportunities.
25. A society where the rich live in mansions while the poor live in shacks.
26. A dystopia where the government enforces strict social control.
27. A society where the poor are denied access to transportation.
28. A dystopia where the rich control the government.

29. A society where the poor are forced to work for the rich.
30. A dystopia where social class determines your job.
31. A society where the rich live in gated communities while the poor live in ghettos.
32. A dystopia where the government enforces strict social hierarchy.
33. A society where the poor are denied access to education.
34. A dystopia where the rich have all the power and influence.
35. A society where the poor are forced to work in sweatshops.
36. A dystopia where social class determines access to healthcare.
37. A society where the rich live in palaces while the poor live in hovels.
38. A dystopia where the government enforces strict social separation.
39. A society where the poor are denied access to clean air and water.
40. A dystopia where the rich control all the wealth.
41. A society where the poor are forced to serve the rich.
42. A dystopia where social class determines your future.
43. A society where the rich live in splendor while the poor live in misery.
44. A dystopia where the government enforces strict social divisions.

45. A society where the poor are denied access to basic necessities.
46. A dystopia where the rich have all the resources.
47. A society where the poor are forced to live in overcrowded conditions.
48. A dystopia where social class determines access to safety.
49. A society where the rich live in grandeur while the poor live in destitution.
50. A dystopia where the government enforces strict social stratification.
51. A society where the poor are denied access to healthcare.
52. A dystopia where the rich control all the industries.
53. A society where the poor are forced to work in hazardous conditions.
54. A dystopia where social class determines your access to justice.
55. A society where the rich live in comfort while the poor live in discomfort.
56. A dystopia where the government enforces strict social control.
57. A society where the poor are denied access to education.
58. A dystopia where the rich have all the influence.
59. A society where the poor are forced to work in dangerous jobs.
60. A dystopia where social class determines your quality of life.
61. A society where the rich live in luxury while the poor live in poverty.

62. A dystopia where the government enforces strict social hierarchy.
63. A society where the poor are denied access to clean water and food.
64. A dystopia where the rich control the media.
65. A society where the poor are forced to work in menial jobs.
66. A dystopia where social class determines your access to healthcare.
67. A society where the rich live in opulence while the poor live in squalor.
68. A dystopia where the government enforces strict social order.
69. A society where the poor are denied access to education and opportunities.
70. A dystopia where the rich control all the resources.
71. A society where the poor are forced to work in dangerous environments.
72. A dystopia where social class determines your future prospects.
73. A society where the rich live in grandeur while the poor live in deprivation.
74. A dystopia where the government enforces strict social segregation.
75. A society where the poor are denied access to basic amenities.
76. A dystopia where the rich have all the privileges.
77. A society where the poor are forced to work for the rich.
78. A dystopia where social class determines your fate.

79. A society where the rich live in splendor while the poor live in hardship.
80. A dystopia where the government enforces strict social control.
81. A society where the poor are denied access to healthcare and education.
82. A dystopia where the rich control all the industries and businesses.
83. A society where the poor are forced to work in hazardous conditions.
84. A dystopia where social class determines your quality of life.
85. A society where the rich live in comfort while the poor live in discomfort.
86. A dystopia where the government enforces strict social divisions.
87. A society where the poor are denied access to clean air and water.
88. A dystopia where the rich have all the influence and power.
89. A society where the poor are forced to serve the rich.
90. A dystopia where social class determines your access to opportunities.
91. A society where the rich live in luxury while the poor live in poverty.
92. A dystopia where the government enforces strict social hierarchy.
93. A society where the poor are denied access to basic necessities.

94. A dystopia where the rich control all the wealth and resources.
95. A society where the poor are forced to work in dangerous conditions.
96. A dystopia where social class determines your access to safety and security.
97. A society where the rich live in opulence while the poor live in squalor.
98. A dystopia where the government enforces strict social order.
99. A society where the poor are denied access to education and healthcare.
100. A dystopia where the rich have all the privileges and rights.

100 Surveillance State Prompts

1. A society where the government monitors every aspect of citizens' lives.
2. A dystopia where people are constantly watched by surveillance cameras.
3. The government uses drones to track and monitor the population.
4. A society where privacy is a distant memory.
5. A dystopia where the government uses facial recognition to control the population.
6. A society where people are required to report any suspicious behavior.
7. The government uses advanced AI to monitor and control the population.
8. A dystopia where people are required to wear tracking devices.
9. A society where the government controls all forms of communication.
10. A dystopia where the government uses surveillance to suppress dissent.
11. A society where people are required to undergo regular surveillance checks.

12. A dystopia where the government uses surveillance to control behavior.
13. A society where people are constantly monitored by biometric devices.
14. A dystopia where the government uses surveillance to enforce conformity.
15. A society where people are required to carry identification cards at all times.
16. A dystopia where the government uses surveillance to predict and prevent crime.
17. A society where people are constantly watched by government agents.
18. A dystopia where the government uses surveillance to manipulate public opinion.
19. A society where people are required to undergo regular loyalty tests.
20. A dystopia where the government uses surveillance to control thoughts.
21. A society where people are constantly monitored by their own devices.
22. A dystopia where the government uses surveillance to enforce social order.
23. A society where people are required to report their daily activities to the government.
24. A dystopia where the government uses surveillance to suppress free speech.
25. A society where people are constantly watched by their neighbors.
26. A dystopia where the government uses surveillance to control information.

27. A society where people are required to wear surveillance devices at all times.
28. A dystopia where the government uses surveillance to enforce loyalty.
29. A society where people are constantly monitored by hidden cameras.
30. A dystopia where the government uses surveillance to control access to resources.
31. A society where people are required to undergo regular surveillance training.
32. A dystopia where the government uses surveillance to manipulate behavior.
33. A society where people are constantly watched by their own families.
34. A dystopia where the government uses surveillance to enforce obedience.
35. A society where people are required to carry tracking devices.
36. A dystopia where the government uses surveillance to control public perception.
37. A society where people are constantly monitored by their own homes.
38. A dystopia where the government uses surveillance to predict and prevent rebellion.
39. A society where people are required to report any anti-government sentiment.
40. A dystopia where the government uses surveillance to control social interactions.
41. A society where people are constantly watched by their coworkers.

42. A dystopia where the government uses surveillance to manipulate thoughts.
43. A society where people are required to undergo regular surveillance updates.
44. A dystopia where the government uses surveillance to enforce uniformity.
45. A society where people are constantly monitored by their own pets.
46. A dystopia where the government uses surveillance to control education.
47. A society where people are required to carry surveillance devices at all times.
48. A dystopia where the government uses surveillance to enforce loyalty.
49. A society where people are constantly watched by hidden drones.
50. A dystopia where the government uses surveillance to control access to information.
51. A society where people are required to undergo regular surveillance checks.
52. A dystopia where the government uses surveillance to manipulate behavior.
53. A society where people are constantly monitored by their own devices.
54. A dystopia where the government uses surveillance to enforce social order.
55. A society where people are required to report their daily activities to the government.
56. A dystopia where the government uses surveillance to suppress free speech.

57. A society where people are constantly watched by their neighbors.
58. A dystopia where the government uses surveillance to control information.
59. A society where people are required to wear surveillance devices at all times.
60. A dystopia where the government uses surveillance to enforce loyalty.
61. A society where people are constantly monitored by hidden cameras.
62. A dystopia where the government uses surveillance to control access to resources.
63. A society where people are required to undergo regular surveillance training.
64. A dystopia where the government uses surveillance to manipulate behavior.
65. A society where people are constantly watched by their own families.
66. A dystopia where the government uses surveillance to enforce obedience.
67. A society where people are required to carry tracking devices.
68. A dystopia where the government uses surveillance to control public perception.
69. A society where people are constantly monitored by their own homes.
70. A dystopia where the government uses surveillance to predict and prevent rebellion.
71. A society where people are required to report any anti-government sentiment.

72. A dystopia where the government uses surveillance to control social interactions.
73. A society where people are constantly watched by their coworkers.
74. A dystopia where the government uses surveillance to manipulate thoughts.
75. A society where people are required to undergo regular surveillance updates.
76. A dystopia where the government uses surveillance to enforce uniformity.
77. A society where people are constantly monitored by their own pets.
78. A dystopia where the government uses surveillance to control education.
79. A society where people are required to carry surveillance devices at all times.
80. A dystopia where the government uses surveillance to enforce loyalty.
81. A society where people are constantly watched by hidden drones.
82. A dystopia where the government uses surveillance to control access to information.
83. A society where people are required to undergo regular surveillance checks.
84. A dystopia where the government uses surveillance to manipulate behavior.
85. A society where people are constantly monitored by their own devices.
86. A dystopia where the government uses surveillance to enforce social order.

87. A society where people are required to report their daily activities to the government.
88. A dystopia where the government uses surveillance to suppress free speech.
89. A society where people are constantly watched by their neighbors.
90. A dystopia where the government uses surveillance to control information.
91. A society where people are required to wear surveillance devices at all times.
92. A dystopia where the government uses surveillance to enforce loyalty.
93. A society where people are constantly monitored by hidden cameras.
94. A dystopia where the government uses surveillance to control access to resources.
95. A society where people are required to undergo regular surveillance training.
96. A dystopia where the government uses surveillance to manipulate behavior.
97. A society where people are constantly watched by their own families.
98. A dystopia where the government uses surveillance to enforce obedience.
99. A society where people are required to carry tracking devices.
100. A dystopia where the government uses surveillance to control public perception.

100 Environmentally Driven Prompts

1. A society where climate change has drastically altered the environment.
2. A dystopia where rising sea levels have submerged coastal cities.
3. A society where extreme weather events are a daily occurrence.
4. A dystopia where the government enforces strict environmental regulations.
5. A society where pollution has made the air unbreathable.
6. A dystopia where natural resources are scarce and controlled by the government.
7. A society where people must live in domed cities to escape the harsh environment.
8. A dystopia where the government enforces population control to manage resources.
9. A society where the land is barren and unable to support life.
10. A dystopia where the government uses environmental disasters to control the population.

11. A society where the oceans are too polluted to support marine life.
12. A dystopia where the government enforces a ban on all non-renewable energy sources.
13. A society where people must wear protective gear to go outside.
14. A dystopia where the government controls access to clean water.
15. A society where deforestation has led to severe climate changes.
16. A dystopia where the government uses fear of environmental collapse to maintain control.
17. A society where the environment is so toxic that people cannot go outside.
18. A dystopia where the government enforces strict regulations on resource consumption.
19. A society where the climate is so unstable that seasons no longer exist.
20. A dystopia where the government uses fear of environmental disaster to justify its policies.
21. A society where the land is so contaminated that farming is impossible.
22. A dystopia where the government enforces a policy of mandatory reforestation.
23. A society where the air is so polluted that blue skies are a distant memory.
24. A dystopia where the government controls access to all natural resources.

25. A society where people must migrate constantly to find livable conditions.
26. A dystopia where the government enforces a ban on all single-use plastics.
27. A society where the oceans are so polluted that marine life is extinct.
28. A dystopia where the government uses fear of natural disasters to maintain control.
29. A society where the environment is so unstable that natural disasters are common.
30. A dystopia where the government enforces a policy of mandatory conservation.
31. A society where the rich live in climate-controlled enclaves while the poor suffer.
32. A dystopia where the government controls access to all forms of energy.
33. A society where the environment is so harsh that survival is a daily struggle.
34. A dystopia where the government enforces a policy of zero waste.
35. A society where the land is so barren that desertification is widespread.
36. A dystopia where the government uses fear of environmental collapse to suppress dissent.
37. A society where the air is so toxic that people cannot breathe without masks.
38. A dystopia where the government controls access to all clean water sources.
39. A society where the climate is so unpredictable that seasons no longer exist.

40. A dystopia where the government enforces a policy of mandatory recycling.
41. A society where the environment is so unstable that natural disasters are frequent.
42. A dystopia where the government controls access to all food sources.
43. A society where people must live in eco-friendly homes to reduce their impact.
44. A dystopia where the government enforces a policy of mandatory renewable energy use.
45. A society where the environment is so harsh that only the strongest survive.
46. A dystopia where the government uses fear of environmental disaster to control the population.
47. A society where the oceans are so polluted that fishing is impossible.
48. A dystopia where the government enforces a policy of mandatory green technology use.
49. A society where the land is so contaminated that farming is no longer viable.
50. A dystopia where the government controls access to all forms of transportation.
51. A society where the air is so polluted that people cannot see the sun.
52. A dystopia where the government enforces a policy of mandatory carbon emissions reduction.
53. A society where the environment is so unstable that earthquakes are common.

54. A dystopia where the government controls access to all healthcare resources.
55. A society where people must grow their own food to survive.
56. A dystopia where the government enforces a policy of mandatory water conservation.
57. A society where the climate is so harsh that survival is a daily struggle.
58. A dystopia where the government controls access to all forms of communication.
59. A society where the environment is so toxic that people cannot go outside without protection.
60. A dystopia where the government enforces a policy of mandatory energy conservation.
61. A society where the oceans are so polluted that marine life is extinct.
62. A dystopia where the government controls access to all educational resources.
63. A society where the land is so barren that food is scarce.
64. A dystopia where the government enforces a policy of mandatory environmental education.
65. A society where the air is so polluted that people cannot see the stars.
66. A dystopia where the government controls access to all transportation resources.
67. A society where the environment is so unstable that natural disasters are frequent.

68. A dystopia where the government enforces a policy of mandatory environmental restoration.
69. A society where the climate is so harsh that only the strongest can survive.
70. A dystopia where the government controls access to all economic resources.
71. A society where the oceans are so polluted that swimming is dangerous.
72. A dystopia where the government enforces a policy of mandatory waste reduction.
73. A society where the land is so contaminated that people cannot grow food.
74. A dystopia where the government controls access to all technological resources.
75. A society where the air is so polluted that people cannot breathe without masks.
76. A dystopia where the government enforces a policy of mandatory environmental protection.
77. A society where the environment is so unstable that floods are common.
78. A dystopia where the government controls access to all recreational resources.
79. A society where people must wear protective gear to go outside.
80. A dystopia where the government enforces a policy of mandatory environmental sustainability.
81. A society where the climate is so unpredictable that survival is difficult.

82. A dystopia where the government controls access to all housing resources.
83. A society where the environment is so toxic that people cannot go outside.
84. A dystopia where the government enforces a policy of mandatory environmental conservation.
85. A society where the oceans are so polluted that fishing is impossible.
86. A dystopia where the government controls access to all social resources.
87. A society where the land is so contaminated that people cannot farm.
88. A dystopia where the government enforces a policy of mandatory environmental restoration.
89. A society where the air is so polluted that people cannot see the sky.
90. A dystopia where the government controls access to all cultural resources.
91. A society where the environment is so unstable that natural disasters are common.
92. A dystopia where the government enforces a policy of mandatory environmental education.
93. A society where the climate is so harsh that only the strongest can survive.
94. A dystopia where the government controls access to all environmental resources.
95. A society where the oceans are so polluted that marine life is extinct.

96. A dystopia where the government enforces a policy of mandatory waste reduction.
97. A society where the land is so barren that food is scarce.
98. A dystopia where the government controls access to all natural resources.
99. A society where the air is so polluted that people cannot see the sun.
100. A dystopia where the government enforces a policy of mandatory environmental sustainability.

100 Artificial Intelligence and Robotics Prompts

1. A society where AI governs every aspect of human life.
2. A dystopia where robots have taken over most human jobs.
3. The government uses AI to monitor and control the population.
4. A society where people rely on robots for everyday tasks.
5. A dystopia where AI is used to suppress dissent.
6. A society where robots are programmed to enforce the law.
7. The government uses AI to manipulate public opinion.
8. A dystopia where people are implanted with AI chips.
9. A society where robots are used to control behavior.

10. A dystopia where AI is used to predict and prevent crime.
11. A society where people rely on AI for decision-making.
12. A dystopia where robots are programmed to enforce conformity.
13. A society where AI controls all forms of communication.
14. A dystopia where robots are used to control access to resources.
15. A society where people are monitored by AI devices.
16. A dystopia where AI is used to manipulate thoughts.
17. A society where robots are used to enforce social order.
18. A dystopia where AI controls access to healthcare.
19. A society where people rely on AI for education.
20. A dystopia where robots are used to control public perception.
21. A society where AI monitors every aspect of life.
22. A dystopia where robots are used to enforce loyalty.
23. A society where AI controls access to clean water.
24. A dystopia where robots are used to suppress free speech.

25. A society where people rely on AI for healthcare.
26. A dystopia where AI controls access to food.
27. A society where robots are used to control information.
28. A dystopia where AI is used to enforce obedience.
29. A society where people are monitored by AI at all times.
30. A dystopia where robots are used to enforce social hierarchy.
31. A society where AI controls access to transportation.
32. A dystopia where robots are used to manipulate behavior.
33. A society where people rely on AI for transportation.
34. A dystopia where AI is used to predict and control the future.
35. A society where robots are used to enforce social norms.
36. A dystopia where AI controls access to education.
37. A society where people rely on AI for food production.
38. A dystopia where robots are used to suppress dissent.
39. A society where AI monitors and controls communication.
40. A dystopia where robots are used to control behavior.

41. A society where people are implanted with AI chips.
42. A dystopia where AI is used to enforce conformity.
43. A society where robots are used to control resources.
44. A dystopia where AI manipulates public opinion.
45. A society where people rely on AI for decision-making.
46. A dystopia where robots are used to enforce loyalty.
47. A society where AI controls access to healthcare.
48. A dystopia where robots are used to suppress free speech.
49. A society where people rely on AI for healthcare.
50. A dystopia where AI controls access to food.
51. A society where robots are used to control information.
52. A dystopia where AI is used to manipulate thoughts.
53. A society where people are monitored by AI at all times.
54. A dystopia where robots are used to enforce social hierarchy.
55. A society where AI controls access to transportation.
56. A dystopia where robots are used to manipulate behavior.

57. A society where people rely on AI for transportation.
58. A dystopia where AI is used to predict and control the future.
59. A society where robots are used to enforce social norms.
60. A dystopia where AI controls access to education.
61. A society where people rely on AI for food production.
62. A dystopia where robots are used to suppress dissent.
63. A society where AI monitors and controls communication.
64. A dystopia where robots are used to control behavior.
65. A society where people are implanted with AI chips.
66. A dystopia where AI is used to enforce conformity.
67. A society where robots are used to control resources.
68. A dystopia where AI manipulates public opinion.
69. A society where people rely on AI for decision-making.
70. A dystopia where robots are used to enforce loyalty.
71. A society where AI controls access to healthcare.

72. A dystopia where robots are used to suppress free speech.
73. A society where people rely on AI for healthcare.
74. A dystopia where AI controls access to food.
75. A society where robots are used to control information.
76. A dystopia where AI is used to manipulate thoughts.
77. A society where people are monitored by AI at all times.
78. A dystopia where robots are used to enforce social hierarchy.
79. A society where AI controls access to transportation.
80. A dystopia where robots are used to manipulate behavior.
81. A society where people rely on AI for transportation.
82. A dystopia where AI is used to predict and control the future.
83. A society where robots are used to enforce social norms.
84. A dystopia where AI controls access to education.
85. A society where people rely on AI for food production.
86. A dystopia where robots are used to suppress dissent.
87. A society where AI monitors and controls communication.

88. A dystopia where robots are used to control behavior.
89. A society where people are implanted with AI chips.
90. A dystopia where AI is used to enforce conformity.
91. A society where robots are used to control resources.
92. A dystopia where AI manipulates public opinion.
93. A society where people rely on AI for decision-making.
94. A dystopia where robots are used to enforce loyalty.
95. A society where AI controls access to healthcare.
96. A dystopia where robots are used to suppress free speech.
97. A society where people rely on AI for healthcare.
98. A dystopia where AI controls access to food.
99. A society where robots are used to control information.
100. A dystopia where AI is used to manipulate thoughts.

100 Political and Social Upheaval Prompts

1. A society where the government is overthrown and chaos ensues.
2. A dystopia where the rich control the government and exploit the poor.
3. A society where civil war has broken out and the population is divided.
4. A dystopia where the government uses propaganda to control the population.
5. A society where political corruption is rampant.
6. A dystopia where the government enforces strict laws to maintain control.
7. A society where the population is oppressed by a tyrannical regime.
8. A dystopia where the government uses fear to suppress dissent.
9. A society where political assassinations are common.

10. A dystopia where the government controls all forms of media.
11. A society where the government enforces a policy of mandatory loyalty.
12. A dystopia where political prisoners are held without trial.
13. A society where the government uses secret police to maintain control.
14. A dystopia where political opposition is punishable by death.
15. A society where the government enforces a policy of strict censorship.
16. A dystopia where the government uses fear of rebellion to maintain control.
17. A society where political corruption is the norm.
18. A dystopia where the government enforces a policy of mandatory surveillance.
19. A society where the government uses propaganda to manipulate public opinion.
20. A dystopia where political dissidents are hunted down.
21. A society where the government enforces a policy of strict social order.
22. A dystopia where political opposition is crushed by force.
23. A society where the government uses fear to control the population.
24. A dystopia where political corruption is widespread.

25. A society where the government enforces a policy of mandatory conformity.
26. A dystopia where the government uses propaganda to control thoughts.
27. A society where political dissidents are imprisoned.
28. A dystopia where the government enforces a policy of strict loyalty.
29. A society where the government uses fear of external threats to maintain control.
30. A dystopia where political corruption is endemic.
31. A society where the government enforces a policy of strict surveillance.
32. A dystopia where the government uses propaganda to manipulate behavior.
33. A society where political opposition is silenced.
34. A dystopia where the government enforces a policy of mandatory obedience.
35. A society where the government uses fear to suppress rebellion.
36. A dystopia where political corruption is rampant.
37. A society where the government enforces a policy of strict conformity.
38. A dystopia where the government uses propaganda to control thoughts.
39. A society where political dissidents are hunted down and eliminated.

40. A dystopia where the government enforces a policy of strict social order.
41. A society where the government uses fear to control the population.
42. A dystopia where political corruption is widespread.
43. A society where the government enforces a policy of mandatory loyalty.
44. A dystopia where the government uses propaganda to manipulate public opinion.
45. A society where political opposition is punished severely.
46. A dystopia where the government enforces a policy of strict censorship.
47. A society where the government uses fear of rebellion to maintain control.
48. A dystopia where political corruption is the norm.
49. A society where the government enforces a policy of mandatory surveillance.
50. A dystopia where the government uses propaganda to control thoughts and behavior.
51. A society where political dissidents are imprisoned without trial.
52. A dystopia where the government enforces a policy of strict social control.
53. A society where the government uses fear of external threats to suppress dissent.
54. A dystopia where political corruption is endemic.

55. A society where the government enforces a policy of mandatory conformity.
56. A dystopia where the government uses propaganda to manipulate public perception.
57. A society where political opposition is crushed by force.
58. A dystopia where the government enforces a policy of mandatory obedience.
59. A society where the government uses fear to suppress rebellion.
60. A dystopia where political corruption is rampant.
61. A society where the government enforces a policy of strict conformity.
62. A dystopia where the government uses propaganda to control thoughts.
63. A society where political dissidents are hunted down and eliminated.
64. A dystopia where the government enforces a policy of strict social order.
65. A society where the government uses fear to control the population.
66. A dystopia where political corruption is widespread.
67. A society where the government enforces a policy of mandatory loyalty.
68. A dystopia where the government uses propaganda to manipulate public opinion.
69. A society where political opposition is punished severely.

70. A dystopia where the government enforces a policy of strict censorship.
71. A society where the government uses fear of rebellion to maintain control.
72. A dystopia where political corruption is the norm.
73. A society where the government enforces a policy of mandatory surveillance.
74. A dystopia where the government uses propaganda to control thoughts and behavior.
75. A society where political dissidents are imprisoned without trial.
76. A dystopia where the government enforces a policy of strict social control.
77. A society where the government uses fear of external threats to suppress dissent.
78. A dystopia where political corruption is endemic.
79. A society where the government enforces a policy of mandatory conformity.
80. A dystopia where the government uses propaganda to manipulate public perception.
81. A society where political opposition is crushed by force.
82. A dystopia where the government enforces a policy of mandatory obedience.
83. A society where the government uses fear to suppress rebellion.

84. A dystopia where political corruption is rampant.
85. A society where the government enforces a policy of strict conformity.
86. A dystopia where the government uses propaganda to control thoughts.
87. A society where political dissidents are hunted down and eliminated.
88. A dystopia where the government enforces a policy of strict social order.
89. A society where the government uses fear to control the population.
90. A dystopia where political corruption is widespread.
91. A society where the government enforces a policy of mandatory loyalty.
92. A dystopia where the government uses propaganda to manipulate public opinion.
93. A society where political opposition is punished severely.
94. A dystopia where the government enforces a policy of strict censorship.
95. A society where the government uses fear of rebellion to maintain control.
96. A dystopia where political corruption is the norm.
97. A society where the government enforces a policy of mandatory surveillance.
98. A dystopia where the government uses propaganda to control thoughts and behavior.

99. A society where political dissidents are imprisoned without trial.
100. A dystopia where the government enforces a policy of strict social control.

100 Control of Information and Media Prompts

1. A society where the government controls all forms of media.
2. A dystopia where the government enforces strict censorship.
3. A society where people are only allowed to access government-approved information.
4. A dystopia where the government uses propaganda to manipulate public opinion.
5. A society where independent journalism is banned.
6. A dystopia where the government monitors and controls all communication.
7. A society where the government uses fear to suppress free speech.
8. A dystopia where the government enforces a policy of mandatory media loyalty.
9. A society where the government uses AI to control information.

10. A dystopia where the government uses propaganda to control thoughts.
11. A society where the government controls access to the internet.
12. A dystopia where the government enforces strict regulations on media content.
13. A society where the government uses fear to control public perception.
14. A dystopia where the government monitors all online activity.
15. A society where the government enforces a policy of mandatory media training.
16. A dystopia where the government uses propaganda to control behavior.
17. A society where the government controls all forms of communication.
18. A dystopia where the government enforces a policy of strict media control.
19. A society where the government uses AI to monitor and control information.
20. A dystopia where the government uses propaganda to suppress dissent.
21. A society where the government controls access to all forms of media.
22. A dystopia where the government enforces strict regulations on information.
23. A society where the government uses fear to manipulate public opinion.
24. A dystopia where the government monitors and controls all communication channels.

25. A society where the government enforces a policy of mandatory media loyalty.
26. A dystopia where the government uses propaganda to control thoughts and behavior.
27. A society where the government controls access to the internet and social media.
28. A dystopia where the government enforces strict regulations on media content.
29. A society where the government uses fear to control public perception.
30. A dystopia where the government monitors all online activity and communication.
31. A society where the government enforces a policy of mandatory media training.
32. A dystopia where the government uses propaganda to suppress dissent and rebellion.
33. A society where the government controls all forms of media and information.
34. A dystopia where the government enforces a policy of strict media control and censorship.
35. A society where the government uses AI to monitor and control information and communication.
36. A dystopia where the government uses propaganda to manipulate public opinion and behavior.

37. A society where the government controls access to all forms of media and communication.
38. A dystopia where the government enforces strict regulations on information and media content.
39. A society where the government uses fear to suppress free speech and dissent.
40. A dystopia where the government monitors and controls all communication channels and online activity.
41. A society where the government enforces a policy of mandatory media loyalty and training.
42. A dystopia where the government uses propaganda to control thoughts and behavior.
43. A society where the government controls access to the internet and social media platforms.
44. A dystopia where the government enforces strict regulations on media content and information.
45. A society where the government uses fear to control public perception and suppress dissent.
46. A dystopia where the government monitors all online activity and communication channels.

47. A society where the government enforces a policy of mandatory media training and loyalty.
48. A dystopia where the government uses propaganda to manipulate thoughts and behavior.
49. A society where the government controls all forms of media and information.
50. A dystopia where the government enforces a policy of strict media control and censorship.
51. A society where the government uses AI to monitor and control information and communication.
52. A dystopia where the government uses propaganda to manipulate public opinion and behavior.
53. A society where the government controls access to all forms of media and communication.
54. A dystopia where the government enforces strict regulations on information and media content.
55. A society where the government uses fear to suppress free speech and dissent.
56. A dystopia where the government monitors and controls all communication channels and online activity.
57. A society where the government enforces a policy of mandatory media loyalty and training.

58. A dystopia where the government uses propaganda to control thoughts and behavior.
59. A society where the government controls access to the internet and social media platforms.
60. A dystopia where the government enforces strict regulations on media content and information.
61. A society where the government uses fear to control public perception and suppress dissent.
62. A dystopia where the government monitors all online activity and communication channels.
63. A society where the government enforces a policy of mandatory media training and loyalty.
64. A dystopia where the government uses propaganda to manipulate thoughts and behavior.
65. A society where the government controls all forms of media and information.
66. A dystopia where the government enforces a policy of strict media control and censorship.
67. A society where the government uses AI to monitor and control information and communication.

68. A dystopia where the government uses propaganda to manipulate public opinion and behavior.
69. A society where the government controls access to all forms of media and communication.
70. A dystopia where the government enforces strict regulations on information and media content.
71. A society where the government uses fear to suppress free speech and dissent.
72. A dystopia where the government monitors and controls all communication channels and online activity.
73. A society where the government enforces a policy of mandatory media loyalty and training.
74. A dystopia where the government uses propaganda to control thoughts and behavior.
75. A society where the government controls access to the internet and social media platforms.
76. A dystopia where the government enforces strict regulations on media content and information.
77. A society where the government uses fear to control public perception and suppress dissent.

78. A dystopia where the government monitors all online activity and communication channels.
79. A society where the government enforces a policy of mandatory media training and loyalty.
80. A dystopia where the government uses propaganda to manipulate thoughts and behavior.
81. A society where the government controls all forms of media and information.
82. A dystopia where the government enforces a policy of strict media control and censorship.
83. A society where the government uses AI to monitor and control information and communication.
84. A dystopia where the government uses propaganda to manipulate public opinion and behavior.
85. A society where the government controls access to all forms of media and communication.
86. A dystopia where the government enforces strict regulations on information and media content.
87. A society where the government uses fear to suppress free speech and dissent.
88. A dystopia where the government monitors and controls all communication channels and online activity.

89. A society where the government enforces a policy of mandatory media loyalty and training.
90. A dystopia where the government uses propaganda to control thoughts and behavior.
91. A society where the government controls access to the internet and social media platforms.
92. A dystopia where the government enforces strict regulations on media content and information.
93. A society where the government uses fear to control public perception and suppress dissent.
94. A dystopia where the government monitors all online activity and communication channels.
95. A society where the government enforces a policy of mandatory media training and loyalty.
96. A dystopia where the government uses propaganda to manipulate thoughts and behavior.
97. A society where the government controls all forms of media and information.
98. A dystopia where the government enforces a policy of strict media control and censorship.

99. A society where the government uses AI to monitor and control information and communication.
100. A dystopia where the government uses propaganda to manipulate public opinion and behavior.

100 Corporate Control and Exploitation Prompts

1. A society where corporations control every aspect of life.
2. A dystopia where the government is controlled by corporate interests.
3. A society where people are forced to work for mega-corporations.
4. A dystopia where corporations exploit the poor for profit.
5. A society where corporate surveillance is ubiquitous.
6. A dystopia where corporations control access to essential resources.
7. A society where people are treated as commodities by corporations.
8. A dystopia where corporate greed leads to environmental destruction.
9. A society where corporations enforce strict social hierarchies.

10. A dystopia where the government enforces corporate policies.
11. A society where people are forced to live in corporate-owned housing.
12. A dystopia where corporations control all forms of media.
13. A society where corporate interests dictate government policies.
14. A dystopia where people are forced to work in dangerous conditions.
15. A society where corporate loyalty is mandatory.
16. A dystopia where corporations control the food supply.
17. A society where people are denied basic rights by corporations.
18. A dystopia where corporations exploit natural resources without regulation.
19. A society where corporate propaganda is widespread.
20. A dystopia where the government enforces corporate laws.
21. A society where people are forced to work for minimal wages.
22. A dystopia where corporations control access to healthcare.
23. A society where corporate interests override human rights.
24. A dystopia where people are forced to live in corporate-controlled communities.

25. A society where corporate surveillance is constant.
26. A dystopia where corporations control all forms of communication.
27. A society where corporate interests dictate social norms.
28. A dystopia where people are forced to work in sweatshops.
29. A society where corporate exploitation is rampant.
30. A dystopia where the government enforces corporate policies.
31. A society where people are treated as expendable by corporations.
32. A dystopia where corporations control access to education.
33. A society where corporate interests dictate public policies.
34. A dystopia where people are forced to live in corporate-owned housing.
35. A society where corporate surveillance is ubiquitous and constant.
36. A dystopia where corporations control access to essential resources.
37. A society where people are treated as commodities by corporations.
38. A dystopia where corporate greed leads to environmental destruction.
39. A society where corporations enforce strict social hierarchies.

40. A dystopia where the government enforces corporate policies and interests.
41. A society where people are forced to work in dangerous conditions.
42. A dystopia where corporations control access to healthcare and education.
43. A society where corporate interests dictate government policies and laws.
44. A dystopia where people are forced to live in corporate-controlled communities.
45. A society where corporate surveillance is constant and pervasive.
46. A dystopia where corporations control all forms of media and communication.
47. A society where corporate interests override human rights and freedoms.
48. A dystopia where people are forced to work for minimal wages and inhumane conditions.
49. A society where corporate exploitation is rampant and unchecked.
50. A dystopia where the government enforces corporate policies and interests.
51. A society where people are treated as expendable by corporations.
52. A dystopia where corporations control access to essential resources and services.
53. A society where corporate interests dictate public policies and social norms.
54. A dystopia where people are forced to work in sweatshops and dangerous environments.

55. A society where corporate exploitation is widespread and accepted.
56. A dystopia where the government enforces corporate laws and policies.
57. A society where people are treated as commodities by corporations.
58. A dystopia where corporate greed leads to environmental destruction and devastation.
59. A society where corporations enforce strict social hierarchies and divisions.
60. A dystopia where the government enforces corporate policies and interests.
61. A society where people are forced to work in hazardous conditions and environments.
62. A dystopia where corporations control access to healthcare and education.
63. A society where corporate interests dictate government policies and laws.
64. A dystopia where people are forced to live in corporate-owned housing and communities.
65. A society where corporate surveillance is constant and pervasive.
66. A dystopia where corporations control all forms of media and communication.
67. A society where corporate interests override human rights and freedoms.
68. A dystopia where people are forced to work for minimal wages and inhumane conditions.
69. A society where corporate exploitation is rampant and unchecked.

70. A dystopia where the government enforces corporate policies and interests.
71. A society where people are treated as expendable by corporations.
72. A dystopia where corporations control access to essential resources and services.
73. A society where corporate interests dictate public policies and social norms.
74. A dystopia where people are forced to work in sweatshops and dangerous environments.
75. A society where corporate exploitation is widespread and accepted.
76. A dystopia where the government enforces corporate laws and policies.
77. A society where people are treated as commodities by corporations.
78. A dystopia where corporate greed leads to environmental destruction and devastation.
79. A society where corporations enforce strict social hierarchies and divisions.
80. A dystopia where the government enforces corporate policies and interests.
81. A society where people are forced to work in hazardous conditions and environments.
82. A dystopia where corporations control access to healthcare and education.
83. A society where corporate interests dictate government policies and laws.
84. A dystopia where people are forced to live in corporate-owned housing and communities.

85. A society where corporate surveillance is constant and pervasive.
86. A dystopia where corporations control all forms of media and communication.
87. A society where corporate interests override human rights and freedoms.
88. A dystopia where people are forced to work for minimal wages and inhumane conditions.
89. A society where corporate exploitation is rampant and unchecked.
90. A dystopia where the government enforces corporate policies and interests.
91. A society where people are treated as expendable by corporations.
92. A dystopia where corporations control access to essential resources and services.
93. A society where corporate interests dictate public policies and social norms.
94. A dystopia where people are forced to work in sweatshops and dangerous environments.
95. A society where corporate exploitation is widespread and accepted.
96. A dystopia where the government enforces corporate laws and policies.
97. A society where people are treated as commodities by corporations.
98. A dystopia where corporate greed leads to environmental destruction and devastation.
99. A society where corporations enforce strict social hierarchies and divisions.

100.   A dystopia where the government enforces corporate policies and interests.

100 Resource Scarcity and Competition Prompts

1. A society where water is the most valuable resource.
2. A dystopia where food is scarce and rationed.
3. A society where energy resources are controlled by the government.
4. A dystopia where people fight for access to clean water.
5. A society where the government enforces strict resource conservation laws.
6. A dystopia where people must compete for limited food supplies.
7. A society where the rich control access to essential resources.
8. A dystopia where people must live off the land to survive.
9. A society where the government enforces a policy of mandatory resource sharing.

10. A dystopia where people must scavenge for resources in a barren wasteland.
11. A society where the government controls access to clean water.
12. A dystopia where people must compete for access to energy resources.
13. A society where the government enforces strict water rationing.
14. A dystopia where people must barter for food and other essentials.
15. A society where the rich hoard resources while the poor suffer.
16. A dystopia where people must live in resource-scarce conditions.
17. A society where the government controls access to all resources.
18. A dystopia where people must compete for limited medical supplies.
19. A society where the government enforces strict resource allocation.
20. A dystopia where people must scavenge for food and water.
21. A society where the rich have access to abundant resources.
22. A dystopia where people must live in resource-deprived environments.
23. A society where the government controls access to food and water.
24. A dystopia where people must compete for limited energy supplies.

25. A society where the government enforces strict food rationing.
26. A dystopia where people must barter for medical supplies.
27. A society where the rich control access to clean water.
28. A dystopia where people must live in resource-limited conditions.
29. A society where the government enforces a policy of resource conservation.
30. A dystopia where people must scavenge for energy resources.
31. A society where the government controls access to all essential resources.
32. A dystopia where people must compete for limited food and water.
33. A society where the government enforces strict energy rationing.
34. A dystopia where people must barter for essential supplies.
35. A society where the rich hoard food while the poor starve.
36. A dystopia where people must live in resource-scarce conditions.
37. A society where the government controls access to medical supplies.
38. A dystopia where people must compete for limited clean water.
39. A society where the government enforces strict resource allocation policies.

40. A dystopia where people must scavenge for food and medical supplies.
41. A society where the rich have access to abundant clean water.
42. A dystopia where people must live in resource-deprived environments.
43. A society where the government controls access to energy resources.
44. A dystopia where people must compete for limited medical supplies.
45. A society where the government enforces strict water rationing policies.
46. A dystopia where people must barter for food and water.
47. A society where the rich control access to all essential resources.
48. A dystopia where people must live in resource-limited conditions.
49. A society where the government enforces a policy of resource conservation.
50. A dystopia where people must scavenge for energy resources and medical supplies.
51. A society where the government controls access to all essential resources.
52. A dystopia where people must compete for limited food and water supplies.
53. A society where the government enforces strict energy rationing policies.
54. A dystopia where people must barter for medical and food supplies.

55. A society where the rich hoard resources while the poor suffer.
56. A dystopia where people must live in resource-deprived environments.
57. A society where the government controls access to clean water and energy resources.
58. A dystopia where people must compete for limited medical and food supplies.
59. A society where the government enforces strict resource allocation policies.
60. A dystopia where people must scavenge for food, water, and medical supplies.
61. A society where the rich have access to abundant resources while the poor struggle.
62. A dystopia where people must live in resource-limited conditions.
63. A society where the government controls access to all essential resources.
64. A dystopia where people must compete for limited food, water, and energy supplies.
65. A society where the government enforces strict resource conservation policies.
66. A dystopia where people must barter for medical and food supplies.
67. A society where the rich hoard resources while the poor suffer.
68. A dystopia where people must live in resource-deprived environments.
69. A society where the government controls access to clean water and energy resources.

70. A dystopia where people must compete for limited medical and food supplies.
71. A society where the government enforces strict resource allocation policies.
72. A dystopia where people must scavenge for food, water, and medical supplies.
73. A society where the rich have access to abundant resources while the poor struggle.
74. A dystopia where people must live in resource-limited conditions.
75. A society where the government controls access to all essential resources.
76. A dystopia where people must compete for limited food, water, and energy supplies.
77. A society where the government enforces strict resource conservation policies.
78. A dystopia where people must barter for medical and food supplies.
79. A society where the rich hoard resources while the poor suffer.
80. A dystopia where people must live in resource-deprived environments.
81. A society where the government controls access to clean water and energy resources.
82. A dystopia where people must compete for limited medical and food supplies.
83. A society where the government enforces strict resource allocation policies.
84. A dystopia where people must scavenge for food, water, and medical supplies.

85. A society where the rich have access to abundant resources while the poor struggle.
86. A dystopia where people must live in resource-limited conditions.
87. A society where the government controls access to all essential resources.
88. A dystopia where people must compete for limited food, water, and energy supplies.
89. A society where the government enforces strict resource conservation policies.
90. A dystopia where people must barter for medical and food supplies.
91. A society where the rich hoard resources while the poor suffer.
92. A dystopia where people must live in resource-deprived environments.
93. A society where the government controls access to clean water and energy resources.
94. A dystopia where people must compete for limited medical and food supplies.
95. A society where the government enforces strict resource allocation policies.
96. A dystopia where people must scavenge for food, water, and medical supplies.
97. A society where the rich have access to abundant resources while the poor struggle.
98. A dystopia where people must live in resource-limited conditions.
99. A society where the government controls access to all essential resources.

100.   A dystopia where people must compete for limited food, water, and energy supplies.

100 Education and Indoctrination Prompts

1. A society where the government controls all forms of education.
2. A dystopia where children are indoctrinated from a young age.
3. A society where independent thought is discouraged in schools.
4. A dystopia where the government enforces strict educational conformity.
5. A society where critical thinking is suppressed in favor of obedience.
6. A dystopia where the government controls access to educational materials.
7. A society where schools are used to indoctrinate loyalty to the government.
8. A dystopia where the government enforces a policy of mandatory education.
9. A society where dissenting views are not tolerated in schools.

10. A dystopia where the government uses education to control behavior.
11. A society where the government enforces a policy of strict educational conformity.
12. A dystopia where children are taught to spy on their parents.
13. A society where the government controls all educational institutions.
14. A dystopia where the government enforces a policy of mandatory indoctrination.
15. A society where schools are used to enforce social hierarchies.
16. A dystopia where the government controls access to all forms of knowledge.
17. A society where children are taught to be loyal to the government above all else.
18. A dystopia where the government enforces a policy of educational uniformity.
19. A society where independent thought is considered dangerous.
20. A dystopia where the government uses education to suppress dissent.
21. A society where the government controls access to all educational resources.
22. A dystopia where schools are used to indoctrinate obedience to the government.
23. A society where dissenting views are not allowed in educational institutions.
24. A dystopia where the government enforces a policy of mandatory educational conformity.

25. A society where critical thinking is discouraged in favor of loyalty.
26. A dystopia where the government controls all forms of knowledge and information.
27. A society where schools are used to enforce government policies.
28. A dystopia where the government enforces a policy of mandatory indoctrination.
29. A society where independent thought is considered a threat.
30. A dystopia where the government uses education to control behavior and thoughts.
31. A society where the government controls access to all educational materials.
32. A dystopia where children are taught to be loyal to the government above all else.
33. A society where the government enforces a policy of educational conformity.
34. A dystopia where independent thought is suppressed in favor of obedience.
35. A society where schools are used to indoctrinate loyalty to the government.
36. A dystopia where the government enforces a policy of mandatory education.
37. A society where dissenting views are not tolerated in educational institutions.
38. A dystopia where the government uses education to control behavior and thoughts.
39. A society where the government enforces a policy of educational uniformity.

40. A dystopia where children are taught to spy on their parents and report any dissent.
41. A society where the government controls all educational institutions.
42. A dystopia where the government enforces a policy of mandatory indoctrination.
43. A society where schools are used to enforce social hierarchies and government policies.
44. A dystopia where the government controls access to all forms of knowledge and information.
45. A society where children are taught to be loyal to the government above all else.
46. A dystopia where the government enforces a policy of educational conformity and uniformity.
47. A society where independent thought is considered dangerous and discouraged.
48. A dystopia where the government uses education to suppress dissent and control behavior.
49. A society where the government controls access to all educational resources and materials.
50. A dystopia where schools are used to indoctrinate obedience and loyalty to the government.
51. A society where dissenting views are not allowed in educational institutions.
52. A dystopia where the government enforces a policy of mandatory educational conformity.

53. A society where critical thinking is discouraged in favor of loyalty to the government.

54. A dystopia where the government controls all forms of knowledge and information.

55. A society where schools are used to enforce government policies and social hierarchies.

56. A dystopia where the government enforces a policy of mandatory indoctrination.

57. A society where independent thought is considered a threat and suppressed.

58. A dystopia where the government uses education to control behavior and thoughts.

59. A society where the government controls access to all educational materials and resources.

60. A dystopia where children are taught to be loyal to the government above all else.

61. A society where the government enforces a policy of educational conformity and uniformity.

62. A dystopia where independent thought is suppressed in favor of obedience to the government.

63. A society where schools are used to indoctrinate loyalty and obedience to the government.

64. A dystopia where the government enforces a policy of mandatory education and indoctrination.

65. A society where dissenting views are not tolerated in educational institutions.
66. A dystopia where the government uses education to control behavior and thoughts.
67. A society where the government enforces a policy of educational uniformity and conformity.
68. A dystopia where children are taught to spy on their parents and report any dissent.
69. A society where the government controls all educational institutions and resources.
70. A dystopia where the government enforces a policy of mandatory indoctrination and conformity.
71. A society where schools are used to enforce social hierarchies and government policies.
72. A dystopia where the government controls access to all forms of knowledge and information.
73. A society where children are taught to be loyal to the government above all else.
74. A dystopia where the government enforces a policy of educational conformity and uniformity.
75. A society where independent thought is considered dangerous and discouraged.
76. A dystopia where the government uses education to suppress dissent and control behavior.

77. A society where the government controls access to all educational resources and materials.
78. A dystopia where schools are used to indoctrinate obedience and loyalty to the government.
79. A society where dissenting views are not allowed in educational institutions.
80. A dystopia where the government enforces a policy of mandatory educational conformity.
81. A society where critical thinking is discouraged in favor of loyalty to the government.
82. A dystopia where the government controls all forms of knowledge and information.
83. A society where schools are used to enforce government policies and social hierarchies.
84. A dystopia where the government enforces a policy of mandatory indoctrination.
85. A society where independent thought is considered a threat and suppressed.
86. A dystopia where the government uses education to control behavior and thoughts.
87. A society where the government controls access to all educational materials and resources.
88. A dystopia where children are taught to be loyal to the government above all else.
89. A society where the government enforces a policy of educational conformity and uniformity.

90. A dystopia where independent thought is suppressed in favor of obedience to the government.
91. A society where schools are used to indoctrinate loyalty and obedience to the government.
92. A dystopia where the government enforces a policy of mandatory education and indoctrination.
93. A society where dissenting views are not tolerated in educational institutions.
94. A dystopia where the government uses education to control behavior and thoughts.
95. A society where the government enforces a policy of educational uniformity and conformity.
96. A dystopia where children are taught to spy on their parents and report any dissent.
97. A society where the government controls all educational institutions and resources.
98. A dystopia where the government enforces a policy of mandatory indoctrination and conformity.
99. A society where schools are used to enforce social hierarchies and government policies.
100. A dystopia where the government controls access to all forms of knowledge and information.

100 Everyday Life in a Dystopia Prompts

1. A society where people must follow strict daily routines.
2. A dystopia where the government enforces a policy of mandatory curfews.
3. A society where people are required to wear uniforms.
4. A dystopia where personal relationships are regulated by the government.
5. A society where people are required to carry identification at all times.
6. A dystopia where the government controls access to entertainment.
7. A society where people are required to participate in government-mandated activities.
8. A dystopia where personal freedom is restricted.
9. A society where people are required to adhere to strict social norms.

10. A dystopia where the government enforces a policy of mandatory participation in propaganda events.
11. A society where people are monitored by the government in their homes.
12. A dystopia where the government controls access to communication devices.
13. A society where people are required to report any suspicious behavior.
14. A dystopia where personal privacy is nonexistent.
15. A society where people are required to follow government-mandated diets.
16. A dystopia where the government controls access to healthcare.
17. A society where people are required to participate in daily loyalty tests.
18. A dystopia where personal expression is suppressed.
19. A society where people are required to adhere to strict dress codes.
20. A dystopia where the government enforces a policy of mandatory social participation.
21. A society where people are monitored by the government in their workplaces.
22. A dystopia where the government controls access to travel.
23. A society where people are required to follow government-approved schedules.
24. A dystopia where personal freedom is limited by government regulations.

25. A society where people are required to participate in government-approved hobbies.
26. A dystopia where the government controls access to education.
27. A society where people are required to adhere to government-mandated behaviors.
28. A dystopia where personal relationships are regulated by the government.
29. A society where people are required to follow strict daily routines.
30. A dystopia where the government enforces a policy of mandatory curfews.
31. A society where people are required to wear uniforms.
32. A dystopia where personal relationships are regulated by the government.
33. A society where people are required to carry identification at all times.
34. A dystopia where the government controls access to entertainment.
35. A society where people are required to participate in government-mandated activities.
36. A dystopia where personal freedom is restricted.
37. A society where people are required to adhere to strict social norms.
38. A dystopia where the government enforces a policy of mandatory participation in propaganda events.

39. A society where people are monitored by the government in their homes.
40. A dystopia where the government controls access to communication devices.
41. A society where people are required to report any suspicious behavior.
42. A dystopia where personal privacy is nonexistent.
43. A society where people are required to follow government-mandated diets.
44. A dystopia where the government controls access to healthcare.
45. A society where people are required to participate in daily loyalty tests.
46. A dystopia where personal expression is suppressed.
47. A society where people are required to adhere to strict dress codes.
48. A dystopia where the government enforces a policy of mandatory social participation.
49. A society where people are monitored by the government in their workplaces.
50. A dystopia where the government controls access to travel.
51. A society where people are required to follow government-approved schedules.
52. A dystopia where personal freedom is limited by government regulations.
53. A society where people are required to participate in government-approved hobbies.

54. A dystopia where the government controls access to education.
55. A society where people are required to adhere to government-mandated behaviors.
56. A dystopia where personal relationships are regulated by the government.
57. A society where people are required to follow strict daily routines.
58. A dystopia where the government enforces a policy of mandatory curfews.
59. A society where people are required to wear uniforms.
60. A dystopia where personal relationships are regulated by the government.
61. A society where people are required to carry identification at all times.
62. A dystopia where the government controls access to entertainment.
63. A society where people are required to participate in government-mandated activities.
64. A dystopia where personal freedom is restricted.
65. A society where people are required to adhere to strict social norms.
66. A dystopia where the government enforces a policy of mandatory participation in propaganda events.
67. A society where people are monitored by the government in their homes.

68. A dystopia where the government controls access to communication devices.
69. A society where people are required to report any suspicious behavior.
70. A dystopia where personal privacy is nonexistent.
71. A society where people are required to follow government-mandated diets.
72. A dystopia where the government controls access to healthcare.
73. A society where people are required to participate in daily loyalty tests.
74. A dystopia where personal expression is suppressed.
75. A society where people are required to adhere to strict dress codes.
76. A dystopia where the government enforces a policy of mandatory social participation.
77. A society where people are monitored by the government in their workplaces.
78. A dystopia where the government controls access to travel.
79. A society where people are required to follow government-approved schedules.
80. A dystopia where personal freedom is limited by government regulations.
81. A society where people are required to participate in government-approved hobbies.
82. A dystopia where the government controls access to education.

83. A society where people are required to adhere to government-mandated behaviors.
84. A dystopia where personal relationships are regulated by the government.
85. A society where people are required to follow strict daily routines.
86. A dystopia where the government enforces a policy of mandatory curfews.
87. A society where people are required to wear uniforms.
88. A dystopia where personal relationships are regulated by the government.
89. A society where people are required to carry identification at all times.
90. A dystopia where the government controls access to entertainment.
91. A society where people are required to participate in government-mandated activities.
92. A dystopia where personal freedom is restricted.
93. A society where people are required to adhere to strict social norms.
94. A dystopia where the government enforces a policy of mandatory participation in propaganda events.
95. A society where people are monitored by the government in their homes.
96. A dystopia where the government controls access to communication devices.

97. A society where people are required to report any suspicious behavior.
98. A dystopia where personal privacy is nonexistent.
99. A society where people are required to follow government-mandated diets.
100. A dystopia where the government controls access to healthcare.

www.ingramcontent.com/pod-product-compliance
Lightning Source LLC
Chambersburg PA
CBHW071024250726
48653CB00005B/1707